Also by Iyanla Vanzant:

Acts of Faith
The Value in the Valley
Faith in the Valley
One Day My Soul Just Opened Up
In the Meantime
Yesterday, I Cried

An Inner Visions Book

Don't Give It Away!

A Workbook of Self-Awareness
and Self-Affirmations for Young Women

Iyanla Vanzant

with Almasi Wilcots

A Fireside Book
Published by Simon & Schuster

F FIRESIDE
Rockefeller Center
1230 Avenue of the Americas
New York, NY 10020

Copyright © 1999 by Iyanla Vanzant

All rights reserved,
including the right of reproduction
in whole or in part in any form.

First Fireside Edition 1999

FIRESIDE and colophon are registered trademarks
of Simon & Schuster Inc.

The symbols decorating this book are from *The Adinkra Dictionary* by
Bruce Willis, published by The Pyramid Complex. Used by permission.

Book design and composition by Diane Hobbing of Snap-Haus Graphics

Manufactured in the United States of America

1 2 3 4 5 6 7 8 9 10

ISBN 0-684-86983-7

This book is dedicated to
the precious and beautiful little girl
who is alive in all women.
And,
to the daughters of the Inner Visions Team:
Nzinga Adelona
Maia Bandele
Aliyah Berry
Simone Brown
Robin Gambrell
Mikki Griggs
Monifa Jones
Rashida Jones
Sakinah Kinard
Niamoja Morgan
Naa Borko Sackeyfio
Naa Borle Sackeyfio
Senita Stillwell-Muhammed
Gemmia Vanzant
Nisa Vanzant
Chisamiso Zulu
Motisola Zulu

A GIRL'S PLEDGE

I am a girl.

I am an expression of beauty, joy, and love.

I have the right, the power and the ability, to create a beautiful, joyful, and peaceful world for myself and others.

I have a body, but I am not my body.

I have a face, but I am not my face.

I am the most important thing in the world to me.

I am love in motion.

I am the light of the world!

I can create!

I can make a mistake!

I can create something beautiful in all that I do.

I deserve the best.

I give my best.

I do my best to always take care of me!

I am a girl!

I am growing into a woman!

I AM IT!

I am the joy the world is waiting for!

YOU Are It!
Never Give Your
Self Away!

Dear One:

You are it! There is nothing in this world more important, more precious, more perfect than you. You are all that you will ever need. You have within you the ability to create all that you desire to be, to have, and to experience. You are the power! You have the power! You are powerful! (GV)

Your parents, your friends, lovers, and loved ones may not be with you forever, but God is always there with you, for you. Others may not be able to answer your questions, soothe your pain, put a smile on your face, or bring peace to your heart, but God can and will. (AW)

Since you will always be with you, because you are so very important to you, you must know how to take care of yourself, how to honor yourself, and how to affirm yourself. My prayer for you is that you know how brilliant and special you are. My prayer is that you realize the world is waiting for you to bring forth all that you are, in the way only you can. (MBD)

Never feel that you have to explain who you are, or defend who you are, or act in ways that please other people if you must dishonor your Self to do so. Just be who you are. You lack nothing. You connect the heavens to the earth in a most sacred way. Your body is the temple. Your heart is the key. Always celebrate the joy that lies within the temple of your heart. (EA)

There will be days, sometimes months or years, when life does not make sense to you. There may be times when you feel terribly afraid, awfully confused, or downright disgusted with yourself and/or your life. This is perfectly normal! All of us who are now "big girls" have been there and done that! (IV) There will also be times when you feel misunderstood and alone. Never dwell on these things. Take time to listen to your heart, spend time with your Self. Avoid at all costs the temptation to place yourself in unhealthy, unproductive, and dishonorable situations just to avoid being alone with the depth of what you feel. (YS) The key is to know that no matter what else is going on in your life, you come first. *You* know what you need. If you have a good relationship with yourself, you will have all that you need to rise to any and every occasion. (IV)

As the days unfold on your life's journey, people, situations, and obstacles may stand in your way. Let your faith be your landmark. At each corner, in every alley, on every path of life, there will be a lamplight, a house light, or a headlight to illuminate your path. Don't try to figure out where the light is leading you, just follow the light! (DS)

No matter what the world or people tell you about yourself, always remember that you are a delicate yet hardy flower. Your true essence will grow, develop, and unfold as the bright blue petals open on a sun-drenched morning glory. Always know that the best is yet to come and that your satisfaction is guaranteed. (JH)

You are God's special gift to the world. You are a bright and shining star. When you look into your eyes in the mirror each morning, tell yourself, *"I am hope! I am joy! I am free! I am happy! I am love! More important, I am me!"* (LG)

You have been loved from the very beginning of your existence. That love is within you. Allow the divine presence of the love within you to shape you, mold you, and direct your life. Listen to your inner voice. Think, act, and speak the truth of who you are, for that truth is always in alignment with the love that is imbedded in your soul. This is the truth that will guide you to abundant fulfillment.

Have fun with life. Keep your life simple. Remember that the little girl in you loves to play. Play, laugh, and always have at least one good friend you can take to lunch. (VB) Work for the joy of it, not just for the money. Always love for the sake of it, not fearing the pain. Give your best! Do your best! Be your best! And, if there is ever a day or time when you cannot figure out what to do, throw your hands in the air and dance! God's angels are your partners. (IV)

Be Blessed, Dear One!
Iyanla Vanzant and the
Inner Visions Mothers

GV—Gemmia Vanzant   JH—Judith Hakima

DS—Danni Stillwell   LG—Lucille Gambrell

AW—Almasi Wilcots   EA—Ebun Adelona

MBD—Muhsinah   YS—Yawfah Shakor

Berry Dawan   VB—Viviana Brown

Let's Get Back to Basics

My

Mind

Is

Mine

I am thinking good, loving thoughts about me!

My

Body

Is

Mine!

I think I am beautiful!
I know I am special!
I take good, loving care of my body!

My
       Feelings
              Are
                    Mine!

I feel good about myself!
I take good care of myself!
I am worth the best of all there is!
Just because I Am!

I Really Do Matter to Me!

Each day, spend a little time doing a little bit, and you will feel and look a lot better.

Find time each day to do each of the following activities.

Give yourself a star, a treat, or something special each day you get it all done because, you really do matter!

Activity	Mon	Tues	Wed	Thu	Fri	Sat	Sun
Quiet Time							
Physical Exercise							
Good Nutritious Food							
School Work/Study							
Fun/Play							
Family Activity							
Something Just For You							
Community Service							
Helpful Reading (Not Just Your Homework ☺)							
Rest and Sleep							

What I Do for Myself Shows Up in My Life as Goodness!

Do You Know Your
ABC's?

Accept your goodness, your beauty, your value, and your worth!

Believe in yourself!

Choose for yourself only those things that are good for you!

Discipline yourself to always do your best and to do it on time!

Excellence, not excess, is the key!

Faith and fearlessness fuel your dreams!

Greatness is the stuff you are made of; act like you know!

Honesty keeps you free of guilt and shame!

Intuition is the teaching from within; pay attention to what you feel!

Joy is what you feel when you love yourself first!

Knowledge is the key to freedom!

Love is what you are, not what you give or get!

Mistakes are lessons that you need to learn!

Never say never! New days bring new ideas and new beginnings!

Order is the law that puts you where you need to be — when you need to be there!

Plan prayerfully. Prepare purposefully. Pursue persistently!

Quiet time is necessary for a powerful mind!

Respect yourself and others will do the same!

Self is the most important thing you have to give!

Trust yourself and the process of life!

Unexpected doors are open!

Victory is the prize!

Wisdom is using what you have!

X-pect the BEST always!

You are the light of the world!

Zealously nurture, honor, and love your self!

You'd Better Recognize!

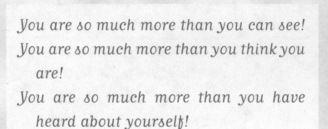

> *You are so much more than you can see!*
> *You are so much more than you think you are!*
> *You are so much more than you have heard about yourself!*

Complete the following sentences with the first thing that comes to your mind about you. Remember to be honest and make sure you think good thoughts. If you can't think of anything to complete the sentence, make it up!

Use your imagination! If your thought is 50 percent believable to you, life will make up the other 50 percent to support you!

Recognize — **YOUR BEAUTY**
I am beautiful because.......................................
....

Recognize — **YOUR POWER**
I am powerful because.....................................
....

Recognize — **YOUR GREATNESS**
I am great because...
....

Recognize—YOUR STRENGTH

I am strong enough to...................................

....

Recognize

Recognize—YOUR TALENTS

I am really good at...................................

....

Recognize—YOUR ABILITIES

I really love to...................................

....

I SEE THE GOOD IN ME!

Recognize

Chillin'

. . . .

Being Alone Is a Special Time

> *There are times when I have special lessons to learn.*
> *The lessons I learn in my quiet time will push me toward my greatness.*

TODAY, I AM WILLING TO CHILL!
To be alone and grow in a special way.

Chillin' is quiet time that you spend getting in touch with how you feel and what you want.

Find a quiet place where you know you will not be disturbed for at least 15 minutes or more.

Play some nice, soothing, instrumental music (music without words) on your Walkman or stereo. If you don't have one of these, a radio will be just fine.

Let your mind wander for a few minutes while you are listening to the music. Try not to focus on any one thing.

Ask your heart to speak to you:

> Dear Heart:
> What is it that I need to know about me today? What is it that I need to know in order to grow to feel good about me? I am listening to you, heart; for all that you reveal to me, I am so grateful!

Use the following pages or your own personal journal to write out your thoughts.

TAKE A LITTLE TIME TO CHECK IN
ON YOURSELF!

Notes from My Heart

I am willing to make
Self-improvements
because I am worth
it!

Notes from My Heart

I am Blessed because
I am The Blessing!

Notes from My Heart

> I am a Divine Idea
> That Is All Good!

Notes from My Heart

I Am a Light
Shining in the
World!

Mirror, Mirror, in My Mind Who Am I?

I have a face!

I am not my face!

My face is a gift that I appreciate!

My face is not the real me!

Fill in the blanks with the first thing that comes
to your mind.

Remember to be honest! If you can't think of
anything you like—

Use your imagination—make it up!

This is between you and you.

No one else is looking.

If it is 50 percent believable to you,

Life will fill in the other 50 percent!

I think my eyes are. . . . .

....

....

I like my eyes because. . . . .

....

....

I think my ears are. . . . .

....

....

I like my ears because. . . . .

....

....

I think my mouth is. . . . .

....

....

I like my mouth because. . . . .

....

....

I think my nose is. . . . .

....

....

I like my nose because. . . . .

....

....

I think my face is. . . . .

....

....

I like my face because. . . . .

....

....

I think my hair is. . . . .

....

....

I like my hair because. . . . .

....

....

I have a body!

I am not my body!

My body is a gift that I appreciate!

My body is not the real me!

Fill in the blanks with the first thing that comes
    to your mind.
Remember to be honest! If you can't think of
    anything you like—
Use your imagination—make it up!
This is between you and you.
No one else is looking.
If it is 50 percent believable to you,
Life will fill in the other 50 percent!

My feet are. . . . .

I like my feet because. . . . .
....
....

My legs are. . . . .

I like my legs because. . . . .
....
....

My waist is. .   .   .   .

I like my waist because. .   .   .   .

My breasts are. .   .   .   .

I like my breasts because. .   .   .   .

My hands are. .   .   .   .

I like my hands because. .   .   .   .

My arms are. .   .   .   .

I like my arms because. .   .   .   .

How Do You See Yourself?

When I look at me, I see· · · · · · ·

....

....

....

....

This makes me feel· · · · · · ·

....

....

....

....

I think the real me is· · · · · · ·

....

....

....

....

How You See Yourself Makes a World of Difference

When you see the good in you
You attract more good to you!

Fill in the blanks with the best things you know
and feel about yourself.

The best thing I know about me is.

I feel good about myself when.

The best thing I can do for myself is.

The thing I want most for myself is. . . .

It's Magic!

When you change your mind about you, everything and everyone changes with you!

Let's Take Another Look

Start small and work your way up to a really
big vision of you!
Fill in the blanks with the first thing that comes
to your mind.
Remember to be honest! If you can't think of anything, use your imagination, make it up!

When I see myself I see. . . . .

. . . .

I like myself because. . . . .

. . . .

When I see myself I see. . . . .

. . . .

I like myself because. . . . .

. . . .

When I see myself I see. . . . .

. . . .

I like myself because. . . . .

. . . .

When I see myself I see. . . . .

. . . .

I like myself because. . . . .

. . . .

I am good at..

I am good because..

I am good at..

I am good because..

I Am Made in the Image of All That Is Good!

I am *really* good at..

I am *really* good because...................................

I am *really* good at..

I am *really* good because...................................

The All Powerful
All Knowing
Creator of All Life
Sees You Just as You Are

God sees me as a beautiful child of life.

God sees me as a beautiful soul.

God sees me as a divine light for the world to see.

God sees me as a purposeful and power-ful person.

God sees me as a strong and courageous person.

God sees me as an intelligent person.

God sees me as love in motion.

God sees love

*Today I see myself as
God sees me!*

God sees good

God sees joy

God sees peace

Today I see myself as God sees me!
Fill in the blanks by using all the things that
God knows about you and sees in you!
If you don't believe it now, keep reading it and
writing it.
What you see, you will soon believe!

I am..

I am..

I am

I am..

I am..

I am

I am..

It's All Good,
And So Am I!

It's All About Me!

What I think,
What I feel,
What I believe about me!

*It is not about what I look like or what I
have.
It's not about my face, my body, or my
clothes.
It is about taking what I have and doing
as much as I can with it.
It is about the business of learning and
growing into the best me I choose to be!
Because I know
It's All About Me!*

Be Who You Are, Perfectly, Because You Are Perfect!

The most perfect thing about me is..................

What Are You
Looking At???

Sometimes, the hardest thing to do is to look at the things I do not like about myself.

It is easy to see those same things in other people, but it is hard to see them in me.

It seems as if the very thing
I cannot see
and don't want to see
about me
keeps showing up around me.

I look at everything around me because
It's all about me.

The thing I don't like about me is......................

I would feel better if...................................

The thing I don't like about me is......................

I would feel better if...................................

The thing I don't like about me is......................

I would feel better if...................................

Do I See the Real Me, or Do I See What Others Think About Me?

Fill in the blanks with the things you know, or ask your family and friends to tell you what they see.

When my mother sees me she sees......................
....
....

When my father sees me he sees.......................
....
....

When my teachers see me they see....................
....
....

When my friends see me they see.....................
....
....

I see the real me!
God knows the real me!

I am the Light of the World
I am beautiful!
I am strong!
I am intelligent!
I am courageous!
I am powerful!
I am great just as I am!

Words Become Things That
You See and Feel!

Re-WRITE each of the following statements while saying them aloud to yourself!

I accept myself just as I am — LOVEABLE!

I accept myself just as I am — POWERFUL!

I accept myself just as I am — COURAGEOUS!

I accept myself just as I am — BEAUTIFUL!

I accept myself just as I am — INTELLIGENT!

I accept myself just as I am — PEACEFUL!

I accept myself just as I am — JOYFUL!

I accept myself just as I am — WONDERFUL!

I accept myself just as I am — DELIGHTFUL!

> *I am blessed!*
> *I am a blessing!*
> *I am a joy to behold!*

I think the truth about me is..............................

This makes me feel..................................

When I think good thoughts, I feel good!

Notes from My Heart

All that I need,
I am!

What Do You Do When You Don't Know What to Do?

A Girl's Survival Kit

There are some things a girl must have if she is to survive being a girl!

The following is a list of items you will find helpful on the days when things aren't going so great.

Ask your friends and relatives to contribute the things you need.

Keep your survival kit in a safe place.

Use your survival kit items when you don't know what else to do to feel better.

Rose-scented bath salts or bubble bath

Lavender-scented bath salts or bubble bath

Peppermint-scented bath salts or bubble bath

A bag of Hershey's Kisses (sugar-free chocolate
is just as good ☺ !)

A fuzzy teddy bear

A Barbie doll with two changes of clothes

A journal or personal notebook

A coloring book and crayons

A purple or blue ink pen

A box of tissues

A bag of peppermint candy (sugar-free candy
is just fine ☺ !)

Your favorite color nail polish (always ask per
mission before you polish ☺ !)

A pink cotton nightgown or pajamas, or a sweat
suit

A white cotton nightgown or pajamas, or a
sweat suit

A set of pink sheets for your bed

2 baby pictures of you

A tree (your tree must be in a place you can get
to quickly and safely. Always ask permission
before you go visit your tree.)

Survival Techniques

The following is a list of things to do when you are not feeling so great.

Try to do at least three of the things on the list, but always take the bath first.

Stay in the bath at least fifteen minutes. (Try not to go outside after bathing ☺ !)

When you finish, you will feel much better!

When you feel angry

Take a rose bubble bath.

Put on your pink nightgown or pajamas, or sweat suit.

Color three pages in your coloring book, and color everything blue and green.

Write out exactly what you are feeling in your journal with your blue pen.

Put the pink sheets on your bed, lie down and curl up with your teddy bear.

When you feel sad

Take a lavender bath.

Put on your best outfit.

Have a Hershey's Kiss or two or three, but no
more than four ☺ !

Color three pages in your coloring book.

After coloring, write out what you feel in your
journal. (Be sure to have the tissues nearby.)

Talk to your baby pictures. Tell the baby all the
things you want to hear.

When you feel confused

Take a peppermint bath.

Suck on a peppermint.

Put on your white nightgown or pajamas, or
sweat suit.

Polish your toenails.

Comb Barbie's hair and change her clothes.

Color three pages in your coloring book.

After coloring, write out what you feel in your
journal.

When you feel frightened

Take a rose or lavender bath. (In an emergency, use a bit of each.)

Have a peppermint candy.

Put on your white nightgown or pajamas, or sweat suit.

Paint your finger and toenails.

Talk to your baby picture. Tell the baby all the things you need to hear.

Talk to your tree. (Get permission before leaving the house.) Tell the tree exactly what you feel, and ask it to help you be strong.

Color five pages in your coloring book. Use as much pink as you can.

When you feel lonely

Take a rose bath.

Put on your pink nightgown or pajamas, or sweat suit.

Have three kisses.

Write a letter to yourself in your journal with your purple pen, explaining why you feel what you feel.

Read the letter to your teddy bear.

Do ten jumping jacks.

Color three pages in your coloring book.

EMERGENCY!
EMERGENCY!

When you feel *really* bad, or if you don't have a survival kit, here's what you can do:

Take a plain old bath.

Suck a lemon.

Do twenty-five jumping jacks.

Look and listen for a bird.

Play with your face and put on makeup. (Always ask permission first ☺.)

Get dressed up in your best clothes.

Write God a letter, explaining how you feel.

Fix your hair a new way.

Watch cartoons.

Review your dream pages (We'll do this later ☺.)

Clean out your closet, desk, drawers, or purse.

Review the first section of this book.

Talk to your baby picture.

Express yourself in your journal or on your "Heart" pages.

Notes from My Heart

I Am Enough!
I Am Good Enough!
I Am Enough to Be
All That I Am

Express Yourself!

Use the following pages to write about your feelings. Write the first thing that comes to your mind. Remember to be honest! This is between you and yourself! No one else is looking!

The thing that really frightens me is

> When you know how much love is inside of you, you cannot be afraid!

I will fear no thing!
Only stars shine in the darkness!
I am not afraid of the dark!
It is my opportunity to shine!
(Repeat this affirmation 21 times whenever you feel afraid.)

The thing that really hurts me is

When I am hurting inside, I look inside for the most powerful medicine I have — My Love!

I plant this hurt in a sea of good thoughts, and it floats away.
(Repeat this affirmation 21 times whenever you feel hurt.)

The thing that really makes me sad is

I stop blaming everyone else for what is not right around me. I learn lessons and let the sadness go!

The waters of peace now wash away sadness.

(Repeat this affirmation 21 times whenever you feel sad.)

The thing that really confuses me is

I am getting clearer and clearer by the minute.

My mind is filled with the wonders of life!
I see everything clearly now!
(Repeat this affirmation 21 times whenever you feel confused.)

The thing that really makes me mad is

I have a choice to
stay mad or
stop being mad and feel better!

Today, I release all anger and replace it with
LOVE.

(Repeat this affirmation 21 times whenever you
feel mad.)

The thing that really makes me happy is

The truth is, I came into this life a winner. No matter what it looks like now, I AM A WINNER!

Happy is what I am!
(Repeat this affirmation 21 times whenever you feel really good.)

I feel really lonely when

There are always
angels watching over
and protecting me.

I am never alone! Angels are always with me!

(Repeat this affirmation 21 times whenever you feel lonely.)

Dear Life:

Take away all the things inside of me
*   that make me feel bad.*

Create in me a clean heart.

Give me a spirit of happiness.

Thank You! Thank You! Thank You!

The things that make me smile are

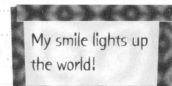

My smile lights up the world!

I am powerful enough to smile the storm clouds away!
(Repeat this affirmation 21 times whenever you need to smile.)

You Must Act as if It Is Impossible to Fail! Because It Is!

Adults want me to stay clean and be quiet.

My teachers want me to do something I don't
really like to do.

My friends want me to do what they want me
to do.

What I really want to do is

I have a loving
goal and a good
purpose in everything
I do!

It Only Takes a Dream!
When You Have a Dream,
Good Things Happen Through You, to You,
and All Around You!

I HAVE A DREAM!

Write a clear statement of your dream. Shoot
for the stars!

Give yourself permission to dream a big dream!
And write it down!

Your written words will be the mold that will
shape your dream!

I dream that one day I will

Now give your dream a shape and form!

Use the next few pages to create a picture of
your dream.

Use a picture of you and pictures from maga-
zines to create your dream world.

Dream Big!

Remember your dream is what you make it!

I Dream a World for Me!

I Dream a World of Good!

I Dream a Life Fantastic!

What's Up??!!!

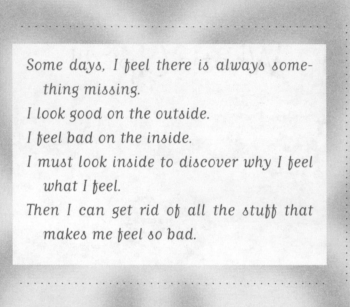

Some days, I feel there is always something missing.

I look good on the outside.

I feel bad on the inside.

I must look inside to discover why I feel what I feel.

Then I can get rid of all the stuff that makes me feel so bad.

I want my inside to feel good and my outside to
look good.

My outside looks good because..........................
....
....

My inside feels bad because.............................
....
....

My inside will feel better when...........................
....
....

Three things I can do right now to feel better
are..
....
....
....

Don't forget your survival techniques!

I feel as good as I look!

I want everything, but nothing makes me
    happy.
When I feel like this,
I must sit down, be still
And think about what I want.
Then,
When I am clear,
I must be brave enough to ask for it.
Patient enough to wait for it.

I choose what I want.
I ask for what I want.
I receive exactly what I ask for.
What I really want is

What Do I Want???

Fill in the blanks with those things you want right now. If you can't identify anything, use your imagination—make it up. Think of all the things that make you feel good.

I really want to...

....

....

This would make me feel..............................

....

....

Three things I am willing to do to get what I want are...

....

....

LET THE GOOD TIMES ROLL!

Today Is a Good Day!

I Am Alive!

I Am Powerful!

I Am Love in Motion!

I Am the Light of the World!

There are times when I want things that may
not be good for me or others in my life.
I can check in with myself to make sure what I
want is going to be good for me.

Take three deeps breaths and ask yourself the
following questions. Write out each answer as
honestly as possible.

Is what I want good for me?.............................
If so, explain to yourself why. If not, explain
why not..

....

....

....

....

Will anyone be hurt or harmed if I get what I
want?...
Explain how everyone involved will be better
or worse off if you get what you want..................

....

....

....

....

Am I ready to handle the responsibility of hav-
ing what I want?..
Explain how and why you are ready..................

....

....

....

....

....

When the time is right,
When I am ready,
All good things will come to pass!

Note from My Heart

> There is nothing
> in the world more
> important to me—
> than me!
> I Am It!

You've Got It
Going On!!

When I take care of myself,
   when I am good to myself,
      when I honor myself and my dreams,
I shine brightly!
I Am a Star!

The following is a list of things that you should
know about yourself.

Complete the list today.

Check the list every six months and see how
much you change and grow.

My favorite color is.....................................

This is my favorite color because.......................

....

....

My favorite food is ....

This is my favorite food because.......................

....

....

....

My favorite song is....................................

This is my favorite song because.......................

....

....

....

My most valued possession is ....

I value this because....................................

....

My greatest strength is ....
I believe this is my strength because................
....
....
My greatest weakness is ....
I believe this is a weakness because.................
....
....
The thing I can do to make my weakness a
strength is..
....
....
My best skill is..
I need the most help in.....................................
....
....
My greatest mistake was ....
I know this was a mistake because....................
....
....
My greatest fear is ....
I fear this because..
....
....
My greatest accomplishment is..........................
....

The thing I am least fond of doing is...............

I don't like doing this because.........................

If my life were to end today, the thing I would
like everyone to know about me is...................

If my life were to end today, the thing I think
others would say about me is............................

If my life were to end today, the thing I would
want everyone to remember about me is...........

If I could start my life all over again, the thing I
would want to be different is.............................

If things were different, I believe I would..........

What's REALLY Going On?

Life is like a puzzle.

Sometimes the pieces fall apart,
but they can be put back together.

There are pieces from your parents and friends, pieces from people you like and from people you don't like that make your life what it is.

There are pieces from books, pieces of songs, and pieces of things that have happened to you.

All the pieces of your life affect you, but THEY ARE NOT YOU!

Label the pieces of your life on the puzzle
below.

Fill in all of the things you feel and think about
your life; make sure to call one piece you.

Color them to show how you feel.

The brighter the color, the better you feel.

Are You Missing Pieces?

Fill in the blanks by writing about the things you feel are missing or are not quite right in your life. Remember to be honest. This is between you and yourself.

The missing piece with my friends is...............

....

....

....

The missing piece at school is...........................

....

....

....

The missing pieces with the adults in my life are...

....

....

....

The piece I am missing is...................................

....

....

....

Stay in Peace,
Not in Pieces!

I can put the pieces of my life together like a puzzle to make a better picture.

Fill in the pieces of the puzzle below with all of
the things you feel are now missing in your
life.

Use your imagination to create what you would
like to see in your life.

Don't forget to include yourself!

*With good thoughts, I can make my life a
better picture.*

I Want Everything, but Nothing Seems to Make Me Happy.

When I feel like this, I must sit down, be still,
and think about what I want.
Then I must be brave enough to ask for it,
and be patient enough to wait for it.

I really want to..

....

....

....

I am ready to..

....

....

....

I am willing to..

....

....

....

I choose and ask, and it is given to me.

Where the Mind Goes, the Behind Follows!

The World I See Is a Picture of My Thoughts.

What are you thinking about?
If you think about only the things you desire,
those are the things that will show up in your
life!

I think life is...

....

....

....

I wish life were ....

....

....

....

I want my life to be......................................

....

....

....

*I can make it happen by changing how I
think about life.*

It is just what I have been thinking about!
I will stop thinking about what I don't want to
happen!
I will stop thinking about what I cannot do!
I will keep my mind on what I want! I will
choose a better life in my own mind because
it's mine!

I choose a life that is ....

....

....

....

I choose friends that make me feel......................

....

....

....

I choose to feel good about myself because......

....

....

....

Notes from My Heart

I Am Whole,
Perfect, and
Complete!

ACT NOW!

If I am afraid to take a chance,
I'll take one anyway.
If I have done things that didn't work out
 well, or that didn't make me feel good,
I will do something else.

I must do something different if I want
 something different to happen.

I am getting better and better!

Habits are the things I do without thinking about them.
When I don't think,
I don't do my best,
and I don't get my best.

There Is Always Room for Improvement

Fill in the blanks with your most honest answer.

Take your time. Think hard. Give it your best so that you will be in touch with your Self.

I made a mistake when I...................................

....

Now that I know better, I can.........................

....

I made a mistake when I...................................

....

Now that I know better, I can.........................

....

I made a mistake when I...................................

....

Now that I know better, I can.........................

....

I made a mistake when I...................................

....

Now that I know better, I can.........................

....

I forgive myself for believing a mistake is a bad thing!

I change my thoughts and actions from good

                to better

                        to the best.

I have the right to make mistakes!
No matter how bad I think I am or how bad I believe I have been—
I can clean out my mind and start again!

Let's Get It On!

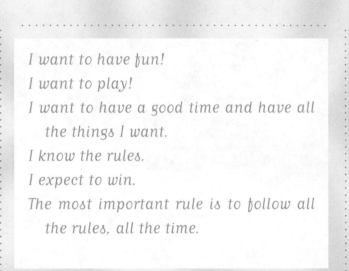

I want to have fun!
I want to play!
I want to have a good time and have all the things I want.
I know the rules.
I expect to win.
The most important rule is to follow all the rules, all the time.

When I play by the rules, I win.

Life's Rules

Love Yourself!
Tell Yourself the Truth!
Tell the Truth to Everyone All of the Time!
Take Care of Yourself First!
Don't Stay Mad More Than Five Minutes!
Do All Things in Love!

When I Play by the Rules I Win!

Dear Self:

I love you today!
I honor you today!
I respect you today!
Today, I intend to take good care of you.
Today, I intend to do everything in my power to
  make sure that you have the best day you
  have ever had.
Today, I will do everything I can to make sure
  that you grow
  and shine
  and have a good time.
Today, I realize that I Am It!
For this I am so grateful!

Inner Visions Worldwide Network, Inc.
926 Philadelphia Avenue, Silver Spring, MD 20910
Phone 301.608.8750 Fax 301.608.3813

We invite you to become a member of the Inner Visions Spiritual Life Maintenance Network and tap into your power.

As a network member you will. . .
• Learn how to consciously apply spiritual principles to your life.
• Learn how to use affirmative prayer to create a shift in your life.
• Learn how to start and maintain a support group.
• Receive a bi-monthly newsletter and soul-work assignment.
• 24-hour access to our prayer line.
• Receive a 10% membership discount to all Inner Visions Activities and workshops.
• Receive 10% discount on all purchases made through Inner Visions.

Annual Dues $37.50 U.S.
(Please call for international rates)

Name_____

Address_____

City_____ State_____ Zip_____

Phone (Day)_____ (Eve)_____

E-Mail_____

Payment ___Check/MO ___Visa ___MC ___AmEx ___Discover

Account Number_____ Exp. Date_____

Cardholders Name _____

Cardholders Signature_____

If you are under the age of 18 please obtain the signature of a parent or guardian for processing authorization _____

Visit our website at http://Innervisionsworldwide.com
E mail: Innervisions@Innervisionsworldwide.com

There Is a Universal Power Seeking an Outlet Through You!

Also available from
Simon & Schuster and
IYANLA VANZANT

Available wherever books are sold.

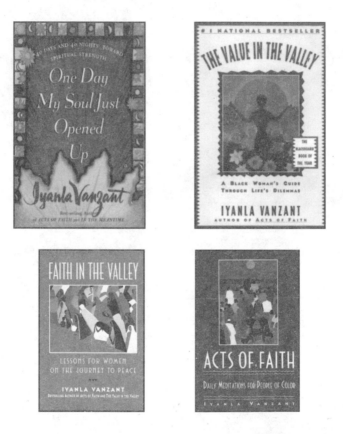